NATIONAL GEOGRAPHIC

Climbing to Success

PIONEER EDITION

By Jacqueline St. Jacques

CONTENTS

CLIMBING TO SUCCESS

Forget gym class. Kili Sherpa's studen

earn how to climb—and survive—Earth's tallest mountains.

BY JACQUELINE ST. JACQUES

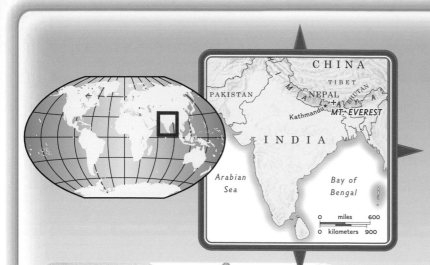

Kili Sherpa always knew he would climb mountains. As a boy, he dreamed of climbing the Himalaya.

These mountains tower over his village. The tallest is Mount Everest. It rises 29,028 feet. It is the highest spot on Earth. Kili wanted to reach its top, or **summit.**

First, he learned to climb. Then he worked as a guide. In 2000, he reached the top of Everest.

He has another job too. It is one he never expected. He is a teacher.

Mountain People

Kili teaches people how to climb mountains. His lessons are free. But they are not for everyone. His school is just for Sherpas.

Sherpas are a group of about 25,000 people. Today, they live in Nepal. They moved there from Tibet in the early 1500s.

From the start, Sherpas respected the mountains. They honored them. The mountains were home to their gods. The one thing Sherpas did not do was *climb* the mountains.

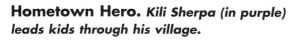

Hometown Hero. *Kili Sherpa (in purple) leads kids through his village.*

Climbing Crews

That changed in the early 1900s. Alexander Kellas came to Nepal. He was a British explorer. He hired Sherpas to carry his gear.

Sherpas started helping other climbers too. One guide became famous. He was Tenzing Norgay. He and a British climber named Edmund Hillary made history. They were the first people to stand on the top of Everest. That was in 1953.

Today, many Sherpas work on the mountain. They can earn a lot of money helping climbers. They set up campsites. They cook meals. They also mark the route up Everest. It is risky work.

Learning the Ropes. *Kili Sherpa (in cap) holds a student's climbing rope (below). That helps students scale the rock safely (right).*

Danger Zone

Everest is dangerous. It has killed more than 150 people. Climbers have died in storms. Some have been killed by **avalanches,** or sliding snow.

No one can make the mountain safe. But good training can help. That is why Kili Sherpa opened his school in 1996.

Wordwise

avalanche: large amount of snow, ice, rock, or dirt that slides down a mountain

belay: to hold a rope for a climber

jumar: to climb a rope with special tools

rappel: to slide down a rope

summit: top of a mountain

Skill + Sense = Safety

Kili wanted to help young Sherpas. Many did not have training. He saw them go on dangerous trips. His school could help them stay safe.

Kili teaches basic climbing skills. He shows students how to tie knots. He teaches them how to climb. The skills include:

- **belaying:** holding ropes so that another climber can move up safely,
- **jumaring:** using rope-gripping tools to climb up, and
- **rappelling:** sliding down a rope.

Peak Opportunities

Students spend days climbing with Kili. They practice the skills over and over. Soon they know the skills by heart. This will help them stay safe on the mountain.

School is just the beginning. Kids learn even more on the job. At first, they do simple tasks. They learn new skills from other climbers. Then they tackle harder jobs. It takes years of training to get ready for a big climb.

Today, many of Kili's students are climbing guides. Some have even worked on trips up Everest.

Kili hopes his students will reach great heights. And he hopes they will come back down again.

Physical Education. *Kili Sherpa's students learn to climb on large rocks.*

The Seven Summits

"The Seven Summits" is the name given to the highest mountain on each continent. Look at the map and chart below to see how these peaks compare.

Mountain	Continent	Elevation	First Climbed
Mount Aconcagua	South America	22,834 feet	1897
Mount Elbrus	Europe	18,510 feet	1874
Mount Everest	Asia	29,028 feet	1953
Mount Kilimanjaro	Africa	19,340 feet	1889
Mount Kosciuszko	Australia	7,310 feet	1840
Mount McKinley	North America	20,320 feet	1913
Vinson Massif	Antarctica	16,067 feet	1966

Scaling Mount Everest

ICE AX: *tool swung into walls of ice, allowing climbers to hold on* ▶

CARABINER: *metal link that connects climbing rope to piton* ▶

PITON: *metal spike driven into rocky cracks to serve as an anchor for ropes* ▼

Making It to the Top
Everest towers above climbers' tents (left). To reach the peak, the climbers rely on these tools of the trade (below).

▲
ICE SCREW: *large metal screw twisted into ice to create an anchor for ropes*

▲
CAM: *device that opens inside a crack, providing an anchor for ropes*

▲
CRAMPONS: *metal spikes that help climbers' boots grip the ice*

The Race

A Peak Experience. *Tenzing Norgay raises a flag at the peak of Mount Everest. He and Edmund Hillary were the first people ever to reach this summit.*

Mount Everest is Earth's highest mountain. For many years, climbing it seemed impossible. But that did not stop people from trying. Many climbers wanted to make history. They dreamed of being the first to the top.

Climbing to New Heights

The race to the top started in the 1950s. Climbers knew they could not make the trip alone. So they formed teams. Team members worked together.

In 1953, two climbers on a British team almost made it. They got close to the peak. Then they had a problem with their gear. They had to turn back.

Two other members tried next. They were Edmund Hillary and Tenzing Norgay. They hiked through the snow. They scaled ice and rocks. Then they did what no one had done before. They climbed to the summit. Hillary reached the top first. Norgay was a few feet behind him.

to the Top

Setting Records

Hillary and Norgay became famous. Soon more people wanted to climb Everest. They wanted to set new records on the mountain.

For 20 years, only men reached the top of Everest. A woman named Junko Tabei changed that.

Tabei was from Japan. She was a music teacher, journalist, and mother. She was also a climber.

In May 1975, she led a team up Everest. It was an all-female team. Tabei became the first woman to reach the summit.

Daring to Climb

Today, people still climb Everest. The journey is dangerous. Yet some people think it is worth the risks. They get to feel what it is like to stand on Earth's highest point.

About 1,600 people have now reached the summit of Everest. More than 70 have been women.

A Female First. *Junko Tabei celebrates on Mount Everest in 1975. She was the first female to stand on the summit.*

Mount Everest

Answer these questions to discover what you learned about Mount Everest.

1 Who is Kili Sherpa?

2 Why did he start a climbing school in 1996?

3 What does Kili teach students?

4 Why is climbing Mount Everest dangerous?

5 What are the Seven Summits? How do they compare?